PRENTICE HALL
WORLD STUDIES
FOUNDATIONS of GEOGRAPHY

Reading and Vocabulary Study Guide

Boston, Massachusetts
Upper Saddle River, New Jersey

The maps on pages 7 and 15 are based on maps created by DK Cartography.

Copyright © 2005 by Pearson Education, Inc., publishing as Pearson Prentice Hall, Boston, Massachusetts 02116. All rights reserved. Printed in the United States of America. This publication is protected by copyright, and permission should be obtained from the publisher prior to any prohibited reproduction, storage in a retrieval system, or transmission in any form or by any means, electronic, mechanical, photocopying, recording, or likewise. For information regarding permission(s), write to: Rights and Permissions Department, One Lake Street, Upper Saddle River, New Jersey 07458.

Pearson Prentice Hall™ is a trademark of Pearson Education, Inc.
Pearson® is a registered trademark of Pearson plc.
Prentice Hall® is a registered trademark of Pearson Education, Inc.

ISBN 0-13-128027-9

9 10   08 07

Table of Contents

How to Use This Book 3

Chapter 1   The World of Geography
Section 1   The Five Themes of Geography 6
Section 2   The Geographer's Tools 9
Chapter 1   Assessment 12

Chapter 2   Earth's Physical Geography
Section 1   Our Planet, Earth 13
Section 2   Forces Shaping Earth 16
Section 3   Climate and Weather 19
Section 4   How Climate Affects Vegetation 22
Chapter 2   Assessment 25

Chapter 3   Earth's Human Geography
Section 1   Population 26
Section 2   Migration 29
Section 3   Economic Systems 32
Section 4   Political Systems 35
Chapter 3   Assessment 38

Chapter 4   Cultures of the World
Section 1   Understanding Culture 39
Section 2   Culture and Society 42
Section 3   Cultural Change 45
Chapter 4   Assessment 48

Chapter 5   Interacting With Our Environment
Section 1   Natural Resources 49
Section 2   Land Use 52
Section 3   People's Effect on the Environment 55
Chapter 5   Assessment 58

© Pearson Education, Inc., publishing as Pearson Prentice Hall. All rights reserved.

Table of Contents

How to Use This Book 3

Chapter 1 — The World of Geography
Chapter 2 — Earth's Physical Geography
Chapter 3 — Earth's Human Geography
Chapter 4 — Cultures of the World
Chapter 5 — Interacting With Our Environment

How to Use This Book

The Reading and Vocabulary Study Guide was designed to help you understand World Studies content. It will also help you build your reading and vocabulary skills. Please take the time to look at the next few pages to see how it works!

The Prepare to Read page gets you ready to read each section.

Objectives from your textbook help you focus your reading.

With each chapter, you will study a Target Reading Skill. This skill is introduced in your textbook, but explained more here. Later, questions or activities in the margin will help you practice the skill.

You are given a new Vocabulary Strategy with each chapter. Questions or activities in the margin later will help you practice the strategy.

Prepare to Read
Section 2 Climate and Vegetation

Objectives

1. Find out what kinds of climate Latin America has.
2. Learn what factors influence climate in Latin America.
3. Understand how climate and vegetation influence the ways people live.

Target Reading Skill

Preview and Predict Before you read, make a prediction or a guess about what you will be learning. Predicting is another way to set a purpose for reading. It will help you remember what you read. Follow these steps: (1) Preview the section title, objectives, headings, and table on the pages in Section 2. (2) Predict something you might learn about Latin America. Based on your preview, you will probably predict that you will learn more about Latin America's climate and plants.

List two facts that you predict you will learn about Latin America's climate and plants.

_____

As you read, check your predictions. How correct were they? If they were not very accurate, try to pay closer attention when you preview.

Vocabulary Strategy

Using Context Clues to Determine Meaning You will probably come across words you haven't seen before when you read. Sometimes you can pick up clues about the meaning of an unfamiliar word by reading the words, phrases, and sentences that surround it. The underlined words in the sentences below give clues to the meaning of the word *dense*.

The Amazon rain forest is *dense* with plants and trees. The plant life is so crowded that almost no sunlight reaches the ground.

Unfamiliar Word	Clues	Meaning
dense	so crowded no sunlight	thick, close together crowded

Chapter 1 Section 2 9

How to Use This Book 3

Section Summary pages provide an easy-to-read summary of each section.

Provides a summary of the section's most important ideas.

Large blue headings correspond to large red headings in your textbook.

This checkmark tells you when to answer the Reading Check question.

Key Terms, in blue within the summary, are defined at the bottom of the page.

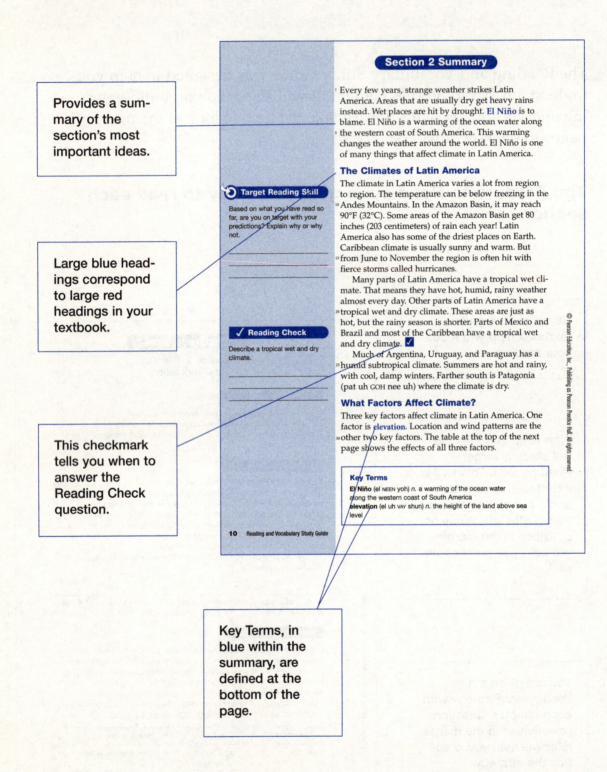

Section 2 Summary

Every few years, strange weather strikes Latin America. Areas that are usually dry get heavy rains instead. Wet places are hit by drought. El Niño is to blame. El Niño is a warming of the ocean water along the western coast of South America. This warming changes the weather around the world. El Niño is one of many things that affect climate in Latin America.

The Climates of Latin America

The climate in Latin America varies a lot from region to region. The temperature can be below freezing in the Andes Mountains. In the Amazon Basin, it may reach 90°F (32°C). Some areas of the Amazon Basin get 80 inches (203 centimeters) of rain each year! Latin America also has some of the driest places on Earth. Caribbean climate is usually sunny and warm. But from June to November the region is often hit with fierce storms called hurricanes.

Many parts of Latin America have a tropical wet climate. That means they have hot, humid, rainy weather almost every day. Other parts of Latin America have a tropical wet and dry climate. These areas are just as hot, but the rainy season is shorter. Parts of Mexico and Brazil and most of the Caribbean have a tropical wet and dry climate. ✓

Much of Argentina, Uruguay, and Paraguay has a humid subtropical climate. Summers are hot and rainy, with cool, damp winters. Farther south is Patagonia (pat uh GOH nee uh) where the climate is dry.

What Factors Affect Climate?

Three key factors affect climate in Latin America. One factor is elevation. Location and wind patterns are the other two key factors. The table at the top of the next page shows the effects of all three factors.

Target Reading Skill

Based on what you have read so far, are you on target with your predictions? Explain why or why not.

✓ Reading Check

Describe a tropical wet and dry climate.

Key Terms

El Niño (el NEEN yoh) *n.* a warming of the ocean water along the western coast of South America
elevation (el uh VAY shun) *n.* the height of the land above sea level

Questions and activities in the margin help you take notes on main ideas, and practice the Target Reading Skill and Vocabulary Strategy.

Causes	Effects
Elevation	The higher the elevation, the colder the temperature
Location	Regions close to the Equator are warmer than those farther away ✓
Wind patterns	Sea breezes keep temperatures mild and bring more rain

Climate, Plants, and People

The Amazon rain forest is dense with thousands of types of plants. The air is hot and moist. In contrast, the Atacama (ah tah KAH mah) Desert in Chile has few signs of life because it is very dry. Latin America's physical features make such climate extremes possible.

Many regions of Latin America have less extreme climates. They have different kinds of vegetation, or plant life. Temperature and rainfall affect what plants grow in a region. They also affect what crops people can grow. For example, sugar cane, coffee, and bananas need warm weather and much rain. These three crops are important in Latin America. The economy of many countries depends on exporting these crops.

Elevation also affects vegetation. The higher the elevation, the cooler and drier it is. Plants must be able to survive in these conditions. ✓

Review Questions

1. What are four climates common in Latin America?
   _____
   _____

2. How does climate affect the people and the economy of Latin America?
   _____
   _____

Key Term
economy (ih KAHN uh mee) n. the ways that goods and services are made and brought to people

---

✓ Reading Check
How does being near to the Equator affect climate?
_____
_____

Vocabulary Strategy
Look at the word *vegetation* in the underlined sentence. Underline the surrounding words or phrases that are clues to the word's meaning.

✓ Reading Check
Describe how elevation affects the vegetation of a region.
_____
_____

Chapter 1 Section 2 11

Use write-on lines to answer the questions. You can also use the lines to take notes.

When you see this symbol, mark the text as indicated.

Chapter 1 Assessment

...ree geographic regions of Latin America are
...exico, Brazil, and Peru.
...e Amazon, the Andes, and the Río de la Plata system.
...iddle America, the Caribbean, and South America.
...ral, isthmus, and tributary.

...mazon River is
...exico's greatest resource.
...e cause of hurricanes in the Caribbean each year.
...xt to the Andes Mountains in Chile.
...e of the largest rivers in the world.

...id subtropical climate is
   A. one in which the weather is hot and rainy all year round.
   B. hot, but the rainy season lasts only part of the year.
   C. similar to the climate in parts of the southern United States.
   D. found in the area called Patagonia.

4. Climate in Latin America is influenced by nearness to the Equator,
   A. vegetation, and the economy.
   B. elevation, and wind patterns.
   C. location, and wind speed.
   D. rivers, and deserts.

5. The amount of natural resources in Latin America can best be described as
   A. the same throughout the region.
   B. similar to that of the United States.
   C. a sign of the region's economic diversity.
   D. uneven from country to country.

Short Answer Question
How does the physical geography of Latin America affect the people who live there?
_____
_____
_____
_____

Chapter 1 Assessment 15

Questions at the end of each section and chapter help you review content and assess your own understanding.

How to Use This Book 5

Prepare to Read

Section 1
The Five Themes of Geography

Objectives

1. Learn about the study of Earth.
2. Discover five ways to look at Earth.

Target Reading Skill

Reread or Read Ahead Have you ever replayed a scene from a video or DVD so you could figure out what was going on? Rereading a passage is like doing this. Sometimes you may not understand a sentence or a paragraph the first time you read it. When this happens, go back and read it again. Sometimes you may need to reread it two or more times.

Reading ahead can help you understand something you are not sure of in the text. If you do not understand a word or passage, keep reading. The word or idea may be explained later.

For example, when you first see the word *degrees* under the heading "Five Ways to Look at Earth," you may not understand what it means. Most people think of how hot or cold something is when they read that word. If you read ahead, you will see that *degrees* is also a unit for measuring angles.

Vocabulary Strategy

Using Context Clues Words work together to explain meaning. The meaning of a word may depend on the words around it, or context. The context gives you clues to a word's meaning.

Try this example. Say that you do not understand the meaning of the word *movement* in the following passage:

> The theme of <u>movement</u> tells you how people, goods, and ideas get from one place to another.

You could ask yourself: "What information does the passage give me about the word?" Answer: "I know that movement is how people, goods, and ideas get from one place to another. This tells me that movement must be a way of getting from place to place."

Section 1 Summary

The Study of Earth and Five Ways to Look at Earth

Geography is the study of Earth. Five themes help geographers keep track of information about Earth and its people. These themes are: **1.** location **2.** regions **3.** place **4.** movement **5.** human-environment interaction. They help us see where things are, and why they are there. ✓

1. Geographers study a place by finding its **location**. Geographers use **cardinal directions** to describe north, south, east, and west.

Another way to describe location is to use latitude and longitude. **Latitude** is the distance north or south of the Equator. **Longitude** is the distance east or west of the Prime Meridian. Latitude and longitude are measured in degrees.

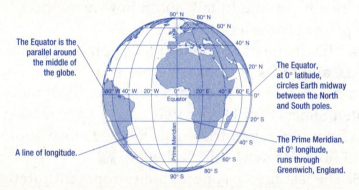

Lines of latitude, also called **parallels**, are east-west circles around the globe. The latitude at 0 degrees (0°) is the Equator. Suppose you could cut Earth in half at the Equator. Each half of Earth is called a **hemisphere**. The Equator divides Earth into Northern and Southern hemispheres.

Key Terms
geography (jee AHG ru fee) *n.* the study of Earth
cardinal directions (KAHR duh nul duh REK shunz) *n.* the directions north, east, south, or west
latitude (LAT uh tood) *n.* the distance north or south of Earth's Equator, in degrees
longitude (LAHN juh tood) *n.* distance east or west of the Prime Meridian, in degrees
parallel (PA ruh lel) *n.* a line of latitude
hemisphere (HEM ih sfeer) *n.* half of Earth

✓ Reading Check

What do the five themes of geography help us do?

_____
_____
_____
_____

Target Reading Skill

Read ahead to see what kinds of things regions can have in common. Pick two to write down.

1. _____

2. _____

Reading Check

What kinds of things go from one place to another in the theme of movement?

_____
_____
_____

Vocabulary Strategy

What does the word *environment* mean in the underlined sentence? Circle the words in this paragraph that could help you learn what *environment* means and write a definition below

_____
_____

Lines of longitude, also called **meridians**, run north and south. The Prime Meridian is the line of longitude that marks 0° of longitude. It divides Earth into Eastern and Western hemispheres.

Lines of longitude and latitude form a global grid. Think of a tic-tac-toe game or a Bingo card. Geographers use this grid to state absolute location. The absolute location of a place is its exact address. For example, Savannah, Georgia, is located at 32° north latitude and 81° west longitude.

2. When places have something in common such as people, history, climate, or land, geographers call them **regions**. For example, the state you live in is a region because there is one government that unites the whole state.

3. Geographers also study **place**. Place includes both human and physical features at a specific location. You might say that the land is hilly. That is a physical feature. Or you might talk about how many people live in a place. That is a human feature.

4. The theme of **movement** tells you how people, goods, and ideas get from one place to another. For example, soccer is a popular game in parts of the United States. People who play soccer have moved here from other countries. This theme helps you understand how and why things change. ✓

5. The last theme is **human-environment interaction**. It looks at how people change the world around them. It also looks at how the environment changes people.

Review Questions

1. What do geographers study?
_____

2. What is a hemisphere?
_____
_____

Key Terms

meridian (muh RID ee un) *n.* a line of longitude

Prepare to Read

Section 2
The Geographer's Tools

Objectives

1. Find out how maps and globes show information about Earth's surface.
2. See how mapmakers show Earth's round surface on flat maps.
3. Learn how to read maps.

Target Reading Skill

Paraphrase When you paraphrase, you put something into your own words. If you can put something into your own words, it means that you understand what you have read. Paraphrasing will also help you remember what you have read.

For example, look at the first paragraph under the heading "Globes and Maps." You could paraphrase it this way:

A globe is the best way to show Earth. The main difference is the size.

As you read, paraphrase the information following each heading.

Vocabulary Strategy

Using Context to Clarify Meaning When you come across a word that you do not know, you may not need to look it up in a dictionary. In this workbook, key terms appear in blue. The definitions of the terms are in a box at the bottom of the page. If you stop to look at the definition, you interrupt your reading. Instead, continue to read to the end of the paragraph. See if you can figure out what the word means from the words around it. Then look at the definition at the bottom of the page to see how close you were. Finally, reread the paragraph to make sure you understood what you read.

Section 2 Summary

Globes and Maps

The best way to show Earth is to use a globe. A globe is a model of Earth with the same round shape. Using globes, mapmakers can show Earth's continents and oceans much as they really are. The only difference is the scale.

There is a problem with globes, though. A globe big enough to show the streets of your town would be huge. It would be too big to put in your pocket.

[Because of that problem, people use flat maps. But maps have problems, too. Earth is round. A map is flat. It is impossible to show Earth on a flat surface without distortion. Something will look too large or too small. Or it will be in the wrong place. Mapmakers have found ways to limit these distortions.] ✓

Where do mapmakers get the information they need to make a map? To make a map, mapmakers measure the ground. They also use photographs taken from planes and satellite images. Satellite images are pictures of Earth's surface taken from a satellite. Both provide current information about Earth's surface.

Geographers also use computer software. A Geographic information system, or GIS, is useful to governments and businesses as well.

Getting It All on the Map

In 1569, a mapmaker named Gerardus Mercator (juh RAHR dus mur KAY tur) made a map for sailors. Mercator wanted to make a map that would help sailors find land. His map showed directions accurately. But sizes and distances were distorted. The Mercator projection is still used today.

Target Reading Skill

Paraphrase the bracketed paragraph in less than 25 words.

_____
_____
_____

✓ Reading Check

What are the advantages and disadvantages of two ways of showing Earth's surface?

Globes

Advantage: _____
_____

Disadvantage: _____
_____

Maps

Advantage: _____
_____

Disadvantage: _____
_____

Key Terms

scale (SKAYL) *n.* relative size
distortion (dih STAWR shun) *n.* loss of accuracy
Geographic information systems (jee uh GRAF ik in fur MAY shun SIS tumz) *n.* computer-based systems that provide information about locations
projection (proh JEK shun) *n.* a way to map Earth on a flat surface

On a globe, the lines of longitude meet at the poles. To make a flat map, Mercator had to stretch the spaces between the lines of longitude. On the map, land near the Equator was about the right size. But land areas near the poles became much larger. <u>Geographers call the Mercator projection a conformal map.</u> It shows correct shapes, but not true distances or sizes.

Another kind of map is named for its designer, Arthur Robinson. The Robinson projection shows most distances, sizes, and shapes accurately. Even so, there are distortions, especially around the edges of the map. It is one of the most popular maps today. ✓

Reading Maps

All maps have the same basic parts. They have a **compass rose** that shows direction. They have a scale bar. It shows how distances on the map compare to actual distances on the land. And they have a **key**, or legend. It explains the map's symbols and shading. ✓

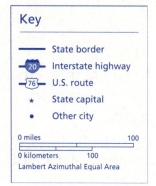

Review Questions

1. Where do mapmakers get the information they need to make a map?
   _____
   _____

2. Which map projection would a sailor most likely use?
   _____
   _____

Vocabulary Strategy

Find the underlined sentence. From context clues, write a definition of *conformal map*. Circle words or phrases in the text that helped you write your definition.

_____
_____
_____

✓ Reading Check

Where is the distortion on a Robinson map?

_____
_____
_____

✓ Reading Check

What do the different parts of a map tell you?

Compass rose: _____
_____

Scale bar: _____
_____

Key: _____
_____

Key Terms

compass rose (KUM pus rohz) *n.* a diagram of a compass showing direction

key (kee) *n.* the part of a map that explains the symbols

Chapter 1 Assessment

1. Which of the following is NOT a tool a geographer would use to study location?
   A. cardinal directions
   B. climate
   C. lines of latitude
   D. degrees

2. The theme geographers use to group places that have something in common is
   A. location.
   B. regions.
   C. place.
   D. movement.

3. What disadvantages do all flat maps share?
   A. They have some sort of distortion.
   B. They are hard to carry.
   C. There are few sources to create them.
   D. They can only show areas at a small scale.

4. Which of the following do mapmakers use to make maps?
   A. ground surveys
   B. aerial photographs and satellite images
   C. Geographic information systems
   D. all of the above

5. What basic parts do all maps share?
   A. compass rose
   B. scale
   C. key
   D. all of the above

Short Answer Question

Which would be more helpful for studying the exact shapes of continents, a globe or a map? Why?

_____
_____
_____
_____

Prepare to Read

Section 1 Our Planet, Earth

Objectives

1. Learn about Earth's movement around the sun.
2. Explore seasons and latitude.

Target Reading Skill

Use Context Clues What should you do when you come across a word you don't know? Or, what if the word looks familiar, but its meaning is unclear to you? Then, look for clues to help you. Context clues are the words, phrases, and sentences around the unfamiliar word.

The word *revolution* is on the next page. Maybe the last time you saw that word it meant a rebellion. In this section, it means something very different. Use the context clues to help you figure out the meaning of revolution.

Vocabulary Strategy

Recognize Signal Words Signal words are words or phrases that prepare you for what is coming next. They are like road signs that tell drivers what to look for on the road ahead. In this section you will learn how Earth travels around the sun. You will also learn how the movement of Earth causes day, night, and the different seasons. Look out for signal words and phrases such as *then, next, as a result, for this reason,* and *as*. They will help you understand how one thing, such as the movement of Earth, leads to another thing, such as why it is morning in New York hours before it is morning in Utah.

Section 1 Summary

Earth and the Sun

The sun is about 93 million miles (150 million kilometers) away. But it still provides Earth with heat and light. If you were to trace the path that Earth makes as it moves around the sun, your finger would trace a circle. Instead of saying Earth circles the sun, we say that Earth **orbits** the sun. It takes one year to complete one **revolution** around the sun.

As Earth orbits the sun, it also turns on its **axis**. Each **rotation** takes about 24 hours. As Earth rotates, it is night on the side away from the sun. As that side turns toward the sun, the sun appears to rise. It is daytime on the side of Earth that faces the sun. As that side turns away from the sun, the sun appears to set. ✓

Earth rotates toward the east, so the day starts earlier in the east. Governments have divided the world into standard time zones. Time zones are usually one hour apart.

Seasons and Latitude

Imagine sticking a pencil through an orange. The pencil is the axis, the orange is Earth. If you tilt or lean the pencil, then the orange tilts too. Earth is tilted on its axis. At different times in Earth's orbit, the Northern Hemisphere may be tilted toward or away from the sun. At other times, neither hemisphere is tilted toward or away from the sun. Earth has seasons because it is tilted during the revolutions.

Let's call the eraser end of the pencil the Northern Hemisphere and the sharpened end the Southern Hemisphere. For several months of the year as Earth orbits the sun, the Northern Hemisphere (eraser end) is tilted toward the sun. The Northern Hemisphere

Reading Check

Explain why it is day on one side of Earth and night on the other side.

_____
_____
_____

Target Reading Skill

Read the underlined sentence. Circle words in the context that tell you what *tilted* means. Write a definition on the lines below.

tilted: _____
_____
_____

Key Terms

orbit (AWR bit) *n.* path one body makes as it circles around another
revolution (rev uh LOO shun) *n.* circular motion
axis (AK sis) *n.* an imaginary line through Earth between the North and South poles, around which Earth turns
rotation (roh TAY shun) *n.* a complete turn

receives lots of direct sunlight. That creates spring and summer in the Northern Hemisphere. At the same time, the Southern Hemisphere (the sharpened end) is tilted away from the sun. The Southern Hemisphere receives indirect sunlight, creating fall and winter in the Southern Hemisphere.

[When the Northern Hemisphere is tilted toward the sun, the Southern Hemisphere is tilted away. For this reason, the seasons are reversed in the Southern Hemisphere.

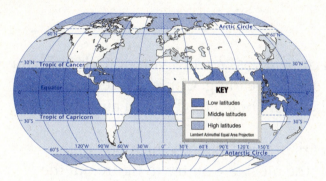

How far a place is from the Equator influences the temperature of a place.Remember that lines of latitude circle Earth above and below the Equator. The areas between the Tropic of Cancer and the Tropic of Capricorn receive fairly direct sunlight all year. Weather is usually hot.

The areas above the Arctic Circle and below the Antarctic Circle get indirect sun. They are cool or very cold all year.

The areas between the high and low latitudes are the middle latitudes. In summer, they get fairly direct sunlight. In winter, they get indirect sunlight. This means they have four seasons. Summers are hot, winters are cold, and spring and fall are in between. ✓

Review Questions

1. What is the rotation of Earth?

_____

_____

2. How do Earth's tilt and orbit cause the seasons?

_____

_____

_____

Vocabulary Strategy

In the bracketed paragraph, a signal phrase is used to show effect. Find the signal phrase and circle it. What effect is explained?

_____

_____

_____

✓ Reading Check

How does latitude influence temperature?

_____

_____

_____

Prepare to Read

Section 2 Forces Shaping Earth

Objectives

1. Learn about the planet Earth.
2. Explore the forces inside Earth.
3. Explore the forces on Earth's surface.

Target Reading Skill

Use Context Clues When you come across a word you don't know, you can often use context to figure out its meaning. Context clues can be a definition, an example, an explanation, or even what you already know about the subject.

The phrase *Ring of Fire* appears in this section. Which box in the graphic organizer will help you the most as you try to figure out the meaning of *Ring of Fire*?

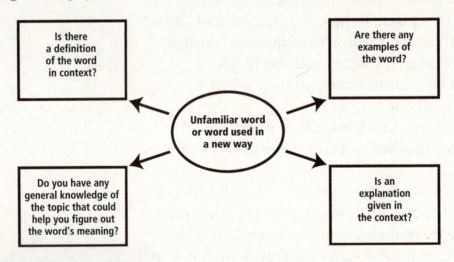

Vocabulary Strategy

Recognize Signal Words When someone drives on a road or highway, road signs can help them know whether to drive fast or slowly, when traffic will merge, and what to watch out for on the road ahead. Recognizing signal words is a lot like reading road signs. Signal words tell you what to expect.

Some signal words show different kinds of relationships, such as contrast. Contrast shows the difference between things or ideas.

Signal words that show contrast include *but, however, not, on the other hand, even though, yet,* and *despite*.

Section 2 Summary

Understanding Earth

Deep inside Earth is a **core** of hot metal. Around that is a second layer called the **mantle**. A third layer floating on top of the mantle is called the **crust**. The surface, or top of the crust, includes Earth's land areas and ocean floors. Powerful forces shape and change Earth. ✓

Most of Earth's surface is not land however. It is water. In fact, water covers more than 70 percent of Earth. The oceans hold about 97 percent of Earth's water. That means that most of Earth's water is salty. Most of the fresh water is frozen. People can use only a small part of Earth's fresh water. It comes from lakes, rivers, and ground water. They receive water from rain.

Above Earth's surface is the atmosphere, a thick layer of gases. The atmosphere contains oxygen that people and animals need to breathe. It also has the gas that plants need.

Earth's land surface comes in all shapes and sizes. Mountains, volcanoes, hills, plateaus, and plains are landforms found on the top of the crust. Mountains rise more than 2,000 feet (610 meters) above sea level. A volcano is a kind of mountain. Hills are lower and less steep than mountains. A plateau is a large, mostly flat area that rises above the land around it. Plains are large areas of flat or gently rolling land.

Forces Inside Earth

Extreme heat deep inside Earth is always changing the way Earth looks on the surface. It makes rocks rise toward the surface. Streams of hot **magma** push up Earth's crust to form volcanoes. Volcanoes pour out molten rock, or lava, from inside Earth.

Streams of hot magma may also push the crust apart along openings called seams. These seams separate

✓ Reading Check

Which layer of Earth contains all of its landforms?

_____
_____
_____

Target Reading Skill

If you do not know what the word *atmosphere* means, notice that a definition follows the phrase in the underlined sentence. What does *atmosphere* mean?

_____
_____
_____

Key Terms
core (kawr) *n.* the sphere of very hot metal at the center of Earth
mantle (MAN tul) *n.* the thick layer around Earth's core
crust (krust) *n.* the thin, rocky layer on Earth's surface
magma (MAG muh) *n.* soft, nearly molten rock

huge blocks of crust called **plates**. A plate may include continents or parts of continents. A plate also includes part of the ocean floor.

35 Sometimes, where two plates meet, molten rock explodes to the surface through a volcano. A good example of this is the Ring of Fire. It is a string of volcanoes near the plates that form the Pacific Ocean. Volcanoes can form at other places, too.

40 When two plates push together, the crust cracks and splinters. These cracks are called faults. When blocks of crust rub against each other along faults, they release energy in the form of earthquakes.

Scientists now know that the forces inside Earth are 45 powerful enough to move continents. They know that the continents were once close together. Magma works to move Earth's plates and continents. ✓

Forces on Earth's Surface

Forces inside Earth slowly build up Earth's crust. But two forces slowly wear down the surface. **Weathering** is one force. Water, ice, and living things like lichens on rocks slowly break rocks into tiny pieces. Weathering helps create soil. Soil is made up of tiny pieces of rock mixed with decaying animal and plant matter.

Erosion also reshapes Earth's surface and land-
55 forms. Water and wind carry soil downstream or downwind to create new landforms. Plains are often made of soil carried by rivers. ✓

Review Questions

1. What are Earth's three main layers?

_____

_____

2. How is erosion different from weathering?

_____

_____

✓ Reading Check

How do continents move apart?

_____

_____

_____

Vocabulary Strategy

In the bracketed paragraph, a signal word is used to show contrast. Find the signal word and circle it. What is being contrasted here?

_____

_____

_____

✓ Reading Check

What is a landform made from weathering and erosion?

_____

_____

_____

Key Terms
plate (playt) *n.* a huge block of Earth's crust
weathering (WETH ur ing) *n.* a process that breaks rocks down into small pieces
erosion (ee ROH zhun) *n.* the removal of small pieces of rock by water, ice, or wind

Prepare to Read

Section 3
Climate and Weather

Objectives

1. Learn about weather and climate.
2. Explore latitude, landforms, and precipitation.
3. Discover how oceans affect climate.

Target Reading Skill

Use Context Clues When you read, you sometimes come across a word you don't know. Sometimes the word you don't know is used in comparison with a word or a group of words you *do* know. These word clues and your own general knowledge can help you figure out what the word means without having to look it up.

Look at this sentence:

The kindling burned more quickly than the other pieces of wood.

Here, the word *kindling* is compared to other pieces of wood. Reading the sentence will help you figure out the meaning of the new word.

Vocabulary Strategy

Recognize Signal Words Signal words are words or phrases that give you clues or directions when reading. Sometimes a signal word or phrase will alert you that two or more things are being compared. Here are some words that can signal a comparison.

also	like	same as
as well as	more	similar to
both	same	too
in the same way	just as	less

Section 3 Summary

Weather or Climate?

Do you check the weather before you get ready for school? Most people need to know the **weather** before they get dressed. They need to know two things. The first is temperature, the second is precipitation. The **temperature** is how hot or cold the air is. **Precipitation** is water that falls to the ground as rain, sleet, hail, or snow. Weather is not the same as climate. Weather is what people feel from day to day. **Climate** is the average weather from year to year. ✓

Why Climates Vary

Earth has many climates. Some climates are so hot that people almost always wear summer clothes. In some climates, snow stays on the ground most of the year. Climate depends on location. Places in low latitudes, or the tropics, have hot climates. This is because they are closer to the Equator and get direct sunlight. Places in the high latitudes, or polar regions, have cold climates. That is because their sunlight is indirect. ✓

Air and water spread heat around Earth as they move. Without wind and water, places in the tropics would overheat. Oceans take longer than land to heat up and cool down. This makes land near oceans have mild temperatures.

Oceans and Climates

An ocean current is like a huge river in the ocean. Ocean currents move across great distances. The currents are huge rivers of warm and cold water. Usually, warm water flows away from the Equator. Cold water moves toward the Equator.

✓ Reading Check

How is climate different from weather?

_____
_____
_____

✓ Reading Check

Which has a colder climate, high latitudes or low latitudes? Why?

_____
_____
_____

Target Reading Skill

If you do not know what ocean currents are, notice that they are compared to huge rivers in the ocean. How does the comparison help you find the meaning?

_____
_____
_____

Key Terms

weather (WETH ur) *n.* the condition of the air and sky from day to day
temperature (TEM pur uh chur) *n.* how hot or cold the air is
precipitation (pree sip uh TAY shun) *n.* water that falls to the ground as rain, sleet, hail, or snow
climate (KLY mut) *n.* the average weather over many years

[Ocean currents help make climates milder. A warm current can make a cool place warmer. A cold current can make a warm place cooler. The warm Gulf Stream gives Western Europe a milder climate than it would if the current was not near. In the same way, the cold Peru Current keeps Antofagasta, Chile, cooler than it would otherwise be.]

Oceans and lakes affect climate in other ways, too. Water takes longer to heat or cool than land. In summer, wind blowing over water cools the nearby land. In the winter, water helps keep nearby land by the shore warmer than inland areas. ✓

Raging Storms

Wind and water can make climates milder. They can also create dangerous storms. **Tropical cyclones** are a good example. Similar storms that form over the Atlantic Ocean are usually called hurricanes. Their winds can reach speeds of more than 100 miles (160 kilometers) per hour. Hurricanes push huge amounts of water onto land, destroying homes and towns.

Tornadoes are like funnels of wind. They can reach 200 miles (320 kilometers) per hour. The swirling winds wreck almost everything in their path. They are just as dangerous as hurricanes. But they affect much smaller areas. ✓

Other storms are less dangerous. In winter, blizzards dump snow on parts of North America. Heavy rainstorms and thunderstorms happen in the spring and summer.

Review Questions

1. What kind of climate occurs near the Equator?

_____

_____

2. How does the ocean influence the temperature of land near it?

_____

_____

Key Terms
tropical cyclone (TRAHP ih kul SY klohn) *n.* an intense wind and rain storm that forms over oceans in the tropics

Vocabulary Strategy

In the bracketed paragraph, a signal phrase is used to make a comparison. Find the phrase and circle it. What is being compared here?

_____

_____

✓ Reading Check

During the summer, are places near the ocean hotter or cooler than places inland?

_____

_____

✓ Reading Check

Which storms cover larger areas, hurricanes or tornadoes?

_____

_____

Prepare to Read

Section 4
How Climate Affects Vegetation

Objectives

1. Investigate climate and vegetation.
2. Explore Earth's vegetation regions.
3. Study vertical climate zones.

Target Reading Skill

Use Context Clues What can you do when you see a word used in an unfamiliar way? Of course, you could look the word up in a dictionary. But often you can get a good idea of what the word means from the words around it.

Textbooks often give examples of new words or ideas. You can tell the meaning of the word from the examples. In the sentence below, the meaning of the word *scrub* is given by the examples in italics:

Scrub includes *bushes and small trees*.

Did you figure out that *scrub* is a word that describes types of plants?

Vocabulary Strategy

Recognize Signal Words Signal words are words or phrases that give you clues or directions when reading. They tell you that what is coming next will be different in some way from what you have just read.

Sometimes a signal word or phrase will help you recognize a cause or effect.

Words that signal causes:	Words that signal effects:
because	as a result
if	so
since	then
on account of	therefore

Section 4 Summary

Climate and Vegetation

These are the five major types of climate: tropical, dry, temperate marine, temperate continental, and polar. Every climate has its own types of natural **vegetation**. That is because different plants need different amounts of water and sunlight and different temperatures to live. ✓

You can probably guess that a **tropical climate** is hot! Some tropical climates also get rain all year long. You would find a tropical rain forest in this climate. Other tropical climates get less rain. In those climates there is more grass and fewer trees.

[**Dry climates** have very hot summers and mild winters. Because dry climates get little rain, few plants can grow there. Semidry climates get just enough rain to grow scrub, including bushes and small trees.]

Temperate marine climates are usually near a coastline. There are three types: Mediterranean, marine west coast, and humid subtropical. All have mild winters. The marine west coast and humid subtropical climates get lots of rain. The Mediterranean climates get less rain and have Mediterranean vegetation.

The summers in **temperate continental climates** can be hot. But the winters are very cold. Grasslands and forests grow in these climates.

Polar climates are always cold. Summers are short and cool there. Winters are long and very cold. In the polar climates you find the **tundra** and ice caps.

Earth's Vegetation Regions

Vegetation depends on climate. But other things, such as soil, also affect vegetation. Geographers have grouped vegetation into several regions. We will study just a few of them here.

✓ Reading Check

Why does each climate have its own type of vegetation?

_____
_____
_____

Vocabulary Strategy

In the bracketed paragraph, a signal word is used to show cause and effect. Find the signal word and circle it. Then write the cause and effect below.

Cause: _____

Effect: _____

Key Terms

vegetation (vej uh TAY shun) *n.* plants that grow in a region
tundra (TUN druh) *n.* an area of cold climate and low-lying vegetation

✓ Reading Check

What types of vegetation grow in deserts?

_____

_____

🎯 Target Reading Skill

Underline the words in the bracketed paragraph that help you to figure out the meaning of the term *coniferous forest*. Then complete the following sentence:

Trees in coniferous forests have _____.

What is the meaning of the word coniferous? What context clues helped you figure out the meaning? Write the context clues on the line below.

_____

_____

✓ Reading Check

How does vegetation change with elevation?

_____

_____

Tropical Rain Forest Plentiful sunlight, heat, and rain cause thousands of plants to grow. The trees grow so tall and close together they form a **canopy** high in the air. Smaller plants grow in the shade.

Tropical Savanna Some tropical areas have less rain. They have a landscape of grasslands and scattered trees known as **savanna**.

Desert Scrub Some very dry areas have just enough rain to support plant growth called **desert scrub**. ✓

Deciduous forest Several different climates support forests of **deciduous trees**. Many people enjoy the changing colors of leaves in the fall.

[**Coniferous forest** Trees with needles instead of leaves can grow in climates that are a little drier than those needed by leafy trees. **Coniferous trees** get their name from the cones they produce.]

Vertical Climate Zones

Mountains have vertical climate zones. That means that climate and vegetation depend on how high the mountain is. In a tropical region, plants that need a tropical climate will grow only near the bottom of a mountain. Farther up you will find plants that can grow in a temperate climate. Near the top you will only find plants that grow in a polar climate. ✓

Review Questions

1. What are the five main types of climate?

_____

_____

2. What landform has a vertical climate zone?

_____

_____

Key Terms

canopy (KAN uh pea) *n.* the layer formed by the uppermost branches of a rain forest

savanna (suh VAN uh) *n.* a parklike combination of grasslands and scattered trees

desert scrub (DEZ urt skrub) *n.* desert plants that need little water

deciduous trees (dee SIJ oo us treez) *n.* trees that lose their leaves seasonally

coniferous trees (koh NIF ur us treez) *n.* trees that produce cones to carry seeds

Chapter 2 Assessment

1. When it is summer in the Northern Hemisphere, it is _____ in the Southern Hemisphere.
   A. summer
   B. winter
   C. spring
   D. fall

2. The layers of Earth include
   A. core, water, crust.
   B. volcanoes, mountains, plateaus.
   C. lava, magma, plates.
   D. core, mantle, crust.

3. Weathering is caused by
   A. water.
   B. ice.
   C. lichens.
   D. all of the above

4. Which of the following influences climate?
   A. latitude
   B. longitude
   C. the Prime Meridian
   D. tornadoes

5. In which vegetation region would you find trees that lose their leaves seasonally?
   A. tropical rain forest
   B. coniferous forest
   C. deciduous forest
   D. tundra

Short Answer Question

Why do some coastal cities in the tropics stay cool?

_____
_____
_____
_____

Prepare to Read

Section 1 Population

Objectives

1. Learn about population distribution.
2. Explore population density.
3. Investigate population growth.

 Target Reading Skill

Comparison and Contrast Have you ever played the game where you try to find the differences between two pictures? The pictures seem to be the same, but if you look closely, you can find little differences. Sometimes the differences are easy to spot. Other times you really have to work at it.

Playing that game is similar to comparing and contrasting as you read. It is easy to see the difference between the terms *birthrate* and *death rate*. But terms like *population density* and *population distribution* will require a little more work.

Vocabulary Strategy

Recognize Roots When you add letters in front or to the end of a root word, you create a new word. You use roots all the time without even thinking about it. When you write, "I watched a movie last night," you knew to add *-ed* to *watch* to create *watched*.

The word *density* appears in this section. The root word is *dense*. The letters *-ity* have been added. But the word isn't spelled *denseity*! It is spelled *density*. Sometimes the root word changes when you add letters. See if you can find more examples as you read. *Hint:* There is one in the first sentence of the next page.

Section 1 Summary

Population Distribution

The way Earth's **population** is spread out is called **population distribution**. People tend to live in uneven clusters on Earth's surface. **Demography** tries to explain why populations change and why population distribution is uneven.

People usually don't move without a good reason. As long as people can make a living where they are, they usually stay there. That means that regions with large populations tend to keep them.

In the past, most people lived on farms where they grew their own food. Therefore, more people lived in places that had good climates for growing crops. After about 1800, things changed. Railroads and steamships made traveling long distances much easier. People moved to cities to work in factories and offices instead of working on farms. ✓

Population Density

How do you find out how crowded a place really is? Find out how many people live in an area. Then divide that number by the area's square miles or square kilometers. That will give you the **population density**. Remember, population distribution tells you the actual number of people in an area. Population density tells you the average number of people in an area.

Some places are more crowded, or have a higher population density than others. For example, Japan has a high population density, while Canada has a low population density. ✓

Key Terms

population (pahp yuh LAY shun) *n.* total number of people in an area
population distribution (pahp yoo LAY shun dis truh byoo shun) *n.* the way the population is spread out over an area
demography (dih MAH gruh fee) *n.* the science that studies population distribution and change
population density (pahp yuh LAY shun DEN suh tee) *n.* the average number of people per square mile or square kilometer

Vocabulary Strategy

Each of the underlined words to the left contains another word that is its root. Circle the roots you find in these words. The root of the first word, *uneven*, is *even*.

✓ Reading Check

What happened to make people move to the cities after 1800?

_____
_____
_____

Target Reading Skill

How is population density different from population distribution?

_____
_____
_____

✓ Reading Check

Which country is more crowded, Japan or Canada? How do you know?

_____
_____
_____

Population Growth

For thousands of years, the world's population grew slowly. Food supplies were scarce. People lived without clean water and waste removal. Millions died of diseases. Although the **birthrate** was high, so was the **death rate**. The life expectancy, or the average length of people's lives, was short.

Today, death rates have dropped sharply. In some countries, birthrates have increased. As a result, populations have grown very fast. At the same time, people live longer than ever. Scientific progress caused much of this change. See the chart below to learn more. ✓

✓ Reading Check

Why have populations risen rapidly in recent years?

_____
_____
_____

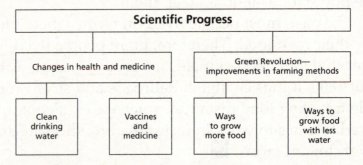

People in many countries still face big problems. Some nations do not have enough fresh water. In parts of Asia and Africa, the population is growing faster than the food supply.

The way people live can be hurt by population growth. There are shortages of jobs, schools, and housing. Public services like transportation and sanitation are inadequate. Forests are disappearing. This causes still more problems.

Review Questions

1. How did the Green Revolution increase population?

_____
_____

2. List problems caused by population growth.

_____
_____

Key Terms

birthrate (BURTH rayt) *n.* the number of live births each year per 1,000 people

death rate (deth rayt) *n.* the number of deaths each year per 1,000 people

Prepare to Read

Section 2 Migration

Objectives

1. Learn about migration, or people's movement from one region to another.
2. Investigate urbanization, or people's movement to cities.

Target Reading Skill

Identify Contrasts Contrast is the way that things are different from each other. Some contrasts are easy to see. For example, it is easy to see how the city is different from the country. The city has more buildings, more people. The country has more plants and trees.

Ideas can be contrasted too. Sometimes it is harder to see the difference in ideas. On the next page you will read about the push-pull theory. Think about how the word *push* means something very different than the word *pull*. This will help you understand the push-pull theory.

Vocabulary Strategy

Find Roots Often, letters are added to the beginning or end of a word. The word the letters are added to is the root word. Sometimes the added letters will completely change the meaning of the root word.

For example, in this section you will study voluntary migration. This is a phrase that means "people choose to migrate." But add the letters *in-* to *voluntary* and you get something very different. *Involuntary migration* is a term that describes people who are forced to move.

Section 2 Summary

Why People Migrate

For thousands of years, people have moved to new places. This movement is called **migration**. **Immigrants** are people who move into one country from another.

Some people choose to move. This is called voluntary migration. Today, most people move by their own choice. The push-pull theory explains voluntary migration. It says that difficulties "push" people to leave. At the same time, the hope for a better life "pulls" them to a new country. ✓

Here is an example of the push-pull theory. Many years ago, 1.5 million people left Ireland for the United States. Disease had destroyed Ireland's main crop, potatoes. Hunger pushed people to migrate. Job opportunities pulled Irish families to the United States.

Today, the main sources of migration are countries where many people are poor or there are few jobs. Sometimes, wars have made life dangerous and difficult. Also, some governments limit people's freedom. These problems push people to leave. They are pulled by the possibility of good jobs or political freedom.

Sometimes people are forced to move. This is known as involuntary migration. In the 1800s, the British sent prisoners to Australia to serve their sentences. War also forces people to migrate to escape death or danger.

The biggest involuntary migration may have been the slave trade. From the 1500s to the 1800s, millions of Africans were enslaved and taken to European colonies in North and South America.

Key Terms

migration (my GRAY shun) *n.* the movement of people from one place or region to another
immigrants (IM uh grunts) *n.* people who move into one country from another

---

✓ Reading Check

Why do people migrate?

_____
_____
_____

Target Reading Skill

How is involuntary migration different from voluntary migration?

_____
_____
_____
_____

Urbanization

Millions of people in many countries have moved to cities from farms and small villages. As a result, some cities have grown <u>enormously</u> in recent years. The movement of people to cities and the growth of cities is called **urbanization**.

In Europe and North America, the growth of industry created jobs. People moved to cities for jobs in factories and offices. Today, people in Europe and North America are moving out of cities into suburbs. Most people in suburbs rely on cars for <u>transportation</u>. More cars mean increased pollution. But people still move to suburbs so they can own homes.

In Asia, Africa, and Latin America, people are still moving from the countryside to <u>growing</u> cities. Indonesia is an example. In the past, people lived in **rural** areas. Recently, many Indonesians have moved to **urban** areas. The capital has grown from 3.9 million people to 11 million people in thirty years. ✓

Often, too many people are moving to the city too fast. Cities cannot provide the things that people need. There are <u>shortages</u> of housing, jobs, schools, and hospitals.

So why do people move to big cities? As hard as life is in the cities, it can be even harder in the countryside. Often, there are few jobs and not enough farmland. Most migrants who move to the city want a better life for their families.

Review Questions

1. Name one push factor and one pull factor.

_____
_____

2. What is urbanization?

_____
_____

> **Key Terms**
> **urbanization** (ur bun ih ZAY shun) *n.* the movement of people to cities, and the growth of cities
> **rural** (ROOR uhl) *adj.* the countryside
> **urban** (UR bun) *adj.* cities and towns

Vocabulary Strategy

Each of the underlined words in the part titled "Urbanization" contains another word that is its root. Circle the roots in these words. The root of the first word, *enormously*, is *enormous*.

✓ Reading Check

How is the population of urban areas changing in Africa, Asia, and Latin America?

_____
_____
_____
_____

CHAPTER 3

Prepare to Read

Section 3 Economic Systems

Objectives

1. Examine different kinds of economies.
2. Investigate levels of economic development.
3. Study global trade patterns.

Target Reading Skill

Make Comparisons Comparing two or more situations lets you see how they are alike. It is often easier to understand new facts by comparing them with facts you already know. Sometimes one thing is compared to several other things.

In this section, you will read about developed nations and developing nations. As you read, compare how people live in developed and developing nations. What kinds of jobs do they have? What kinds of houses do they live in? Do people or machines do most of the work?

Vocabulary Strategy

Recognize Compound Words Compound words are made from two or more words. Compound words are like shortcuts. They make it easier to read or talk about things. For example, *workplace* is a compound word. You could say, "Describe the place where you work." Or, you could say, "Describe your workplace." If you know the meaning of the words that make up a compound word, you can often figure out the meaning of the compound word itself. Here are some compound words you will find in your reading.

sometimes	countryside
worldwide	anybody
healthcare	farmland

Section 3 Summary

Different Kinds of Economies

Economies differ from one country to another. However, in every economy, there are **producers**, who are the owners and workers who make products, and **consumers** who buy and use products.

The owner of the workplace usually decides how and what things will be made. But who are the owners? In some countries, the workplace belongs to private citizens. This economic system is called **capitalism**. In others, the government owns most workplaces. This is called **communism**.

Capitalism is also called a free-market economy. Producers compete freely for consumers' business. People may save money in banks, and invest money in a business.

Under communism, the government controls the prices of goods and services, what things are made, and how much workers are paid. Today, only a few nations practice communism. ✓

In some countries, the government owns some industries while others belong to private owners. This system is sometimes called a mixed economy.

Levels of Economic Development

Three hundred years ago, most people did work by hand. Then people invented machines to make goods. They used energy instead of people and animals to run machines. This was a new form of technology. Technology is a way of putting knowledge to practical use. This change in the way people made goods was called the Industrial Revolution.

Target Reading Skill

Compare producers and consumers. How are they different?

_____
_____
_____

✓ Reading Check

What are two differences between capitalism and communism?

1. _____
   _____

2. _____
   _____

Key Terms

economy (ih KAHN uh mee) *n.* a system in which people make, exchange, and use things that have value
producers (pruh DOOS urz) *n.* owners and workers
consumers (kun SOOM urz) *n.* people who buy and use products
capitalism (KAP ut ul iz um) *n.* an economic system in which individuals own most businesses
communism (KAHM yoo niz um) *n.* an economic system in which the central government owns most businesses

Reading Check

How do developed nations differ from developing nations?

_____
_____

Vocabulary Strategy

The word *healthcare* is a compound word. What are the two root words of *healthcare* and what does each root word mean?

1. _____
   _____

2. _____
   _____

Use the meanings above to understand the meaning of healthcare. Write a definition for healthcare on the lines below.

Healthcare means:

_____
_____

Reading Check

What do developing nations sell to developed nations?

_____
_____
_____

The Industrial Revolution divided the world into **developed nations** and **developing nations**. People live differently in the two types of nations. Developed nations have more industries and a high level of technology. Developing nations have fewer industries and simpler technology. ✓

Only about one fifth of the world's people live in developed nations. These nations include the United States, Canada, Japan, and most of Europe. In these countries most people live in towns and cities. They work in offices and factories. Most people have enough food and water. Most people can get an education and healthcare. Developed nations have some problems. Two of these problems are unemployment and pollution.

Most of the people in the world live in developing nations. These nations are mainly in Africa, Asia, and Latin America. Most people grow just enough food for themselves. People and animals do most of the work. There are many problems in these nations. They include disease, food shortages, and political unrest.

World Trade Patterns

Different countries have different economic strengths. Countries trade with one another to get the things they want and need.

Countries have grown to depend on one another. Developing nations tend to sell foods, natural resources, and simple industrial products. In return, they buy high-technology goods from developed countries. ✓

Review Questions

1. How did the Industrial Revolution change the way people made things?

   _____
   _____

2. How do countries depend on one another?

   _____
   _____

Key Terms

developed nations (dih VEL upt NAY shunz) *n.* nations with many industries and advanced technology

developing nations (dih VEL up ing NAY shunz) *n.* nations with few industries and simple technology

Prepare to Read

Section 4 Political Systems

Objectives

1. Examine different types of states.
2. Investigate types of government.
3. Learn about alliances and international organizations.

Target Reading Skill

Use Contrast Signal Words Signal words are words or phrases that give you clues when reading.

There are different kinds of signal words. Certain words, such as *like* or *unlike, just as* or even the phrase *such as* in the beginning of this sentence can signal a comparison or contrast. This section contrasts several kinds of government. You will learn that some governments encourage people to participate, other governments do not.

In the sentence below, are the signal words signaling comparison or contrast?

Just as in an absolute monarchy, dictatorships do not allow people to participate in government.

Once you read the section you will know for sure!

Vocabulary Strategy

Find Roots Often, syllables or groups of syllables are added at the beginning or end of a word to make a new word.

In some cases, the spelling changes slightly when a word becomes a root. Often, a final *e* is dropped when a new ending is added to a word.

Here are some other examples from this section.

Root	Added letters	New word
make	-ing	making
share	-ing	sharing
simple	-y	simply

Section 4 Summary

Target Reading Skill

The second sentence in the bracketed paragraph begins with the word *Some*. The fourth sentence begins with *Others*. These words signal a contrast. What contrast is made here?

_____
_____

✓ Reading Check

Name four kinds of states.

1. _____
2. _____
3. _____
4. _____

Vocabulary Strategy

Each of the four words below appear in the sections titled "Types of Government," and "International Organizations." Each contains a root that has had a spelling change before the ending was added. Write the full roots on the lines below.

1. earliest _____
2. dictator _____
3. alliance _____
4. organization _____

Types of States

When people lived in small groups, all adults took part in making group decisions. Today, nations are too large for everyone to take part in every decision. But they still need to be able to protect people. They need to be able to solve problems. That is why we have **governments**.

A **state** is a region that shares a government. The entire United States can also be called a state. That's because it is a region that shares a federal government.

[There are four kinds of states. Some regions are **dependencies**. They belong to another state. Others, like the United States, are **nation-states**, which are often simply called nations. Every place in the world where people live is a nation-state or dependency.]

The first states formed in Southwest Asia more than 5,000 years ago. Early cities set up governments called **city-states**. Later, military leaders conquered several countries and ruled them as **empires**. ✓

Types of Government

Each state has a government. There are many different kinds of government. Some are controlled by one person. Others are controlled by all of the people.

The earliest governments were simple. People lived in small groups. They practiced **direct democracy**. All adults took part in decisions. In time, communities banded together into larger tribal groups. Members of the tribe had a say in group decisions. But under **tribal rule**, chiefs or elders made the final decision.

Key Terms

government (GUV urn munt) *n.* a body that makes laws
state (stayt) *n.* a region that shares a government
dependency (dee PEN dun see) *n.* a region that belongs to another state
nation-state (NAY shun stayt) *n.* a state that is independent of other states
city-state (SIH tee stayt) *n.* a small city-centered state
empire (EM pyr) *n.* a state containing several countries

Until about 200 years ago, **absolute monarchy** was one of the most common forms of government. In that system, kings or queens have complete control. Today, there are other countries where just one person rules. The leader is not a king or queen but a **dictator**. Dictators have complete control over a country. An **oligarchy** is a government controlled by a small group of people. The group may be the leaders of a political party, a group of military officers, or even a group of religious leaders. In oligarchies and dictatorships, ordinary people have little say in decisions. ✓

Today, most monarchies are **constitutional monarchies**. The power of the king or queen is limited by law. These nations have constitutions that define the government's power. **Representative democracies** are governments in which people elect representatives who create laws. If they do not like what a representative does, they can refuse to reelect that person.

International Organizations

Nations may agree to work together in an alliance. Members of an alliance are called allies. In some alliances, members agree to protect each other in case of attack. Some alliances, such as the European Union, are mainly economic.

The United Nations is an international organization that tries to resolve problems and promote peace. Almost all of the world's nations belong to the United Nations. It sponsors other international organizations with specific purposes, such as combating hunger or promoting the well-being of children. ✓

Review Questions

1. What were the earliest types of states?

_____
_____

2. What is an alliance?

_____
_____

Key Terms

constitution (kahn stuh TOO shuhn) *n.* a set of laws that define and often limit a government's power

---

✓ **Reading Check**

Name two forms of government in which the leader has total control.

1. _____
   _____

2. _____
   _____

✓ **Reading Check**

What is the purpose of the United Nations?

_____
_____
_____

Chapter 3 Assessment

1. The number of people per square mile or square kilometer is a region's
    A. population.
    B. population density.
    C. population distribution.
    D. life expectancy.

2. People moving to a different region to seek better job opportunities is an example of
    A. urbanization.
    B. suburbanization.
    C. voluntary migration.
    D. involuntary migration.

3. In which of the following does the government control the prices of goods and services?
    A. developed countries
    B. developing countries
    C. capitalism
    D. communism

4. In the earliest societies, the form of government was
    A. direct democracy.
    B. representative democracy.
    C. absolute monarchy.
    D. constitutional monarch.

5. Today, most monarchies are
    A. absolute monarchies.
    B. dictatorships.
    C. oligarchies.
    D. constitutional monarchies.

Short Answer Question

What is the Green Revolution?

_____
_____
_____
_____

Prepare to Read

Section 1
Understanding Culture

Objectives

1. Learn about culture.
2. Explore how culture has developed.

Target Reading Skill

Understand Sequence History is a series of events. To help you understand history, list events in sequence, or the order in which they happened. Make a chart like the one below to help you. This one is about how culture developed. The first two events are filled in for you. Fill in the event that happens next when you come across it as you read. The arrows show how one event leads to another.

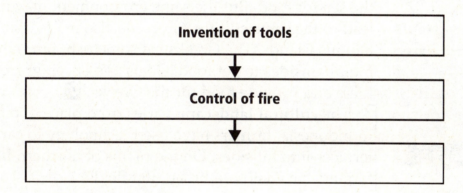

Vocabulary Strategy

Use Context Clues to Determine Meaning Context clues help you figure out the meaning of words. One way to use context clues is to imagine a blank space in place of the word you don't understand. Let's say you don't know the meaning of the word *institutions*. Read the paragraph below. There is a blank everywhere the word *institutions* would appear.

> Before civilizations developed, people had simple _____. These were extended families and councils of elders. As people gathered in larger groups, they needed more complex _____. They developed religions. States needed armies, schools, and governments. Today, we have many different kinds of _____. They are important parts of our culture.

Did you figure out that *institutions* means organized groups of people?

Section 1 Summary

What Is Culture?

Culture is the way people live. It includes what people believe and the things they do everyday. It includes the language people speak and the clothes they wear.

Parents pass culture on to their children. Ideas and ways of doing things are called cultural traits. For example, in the United States, eating with a fork is a cultural trait. In Japan, people use chopsticks.

Some parts of a culture are easy to see. They include houses, food, and clothing. Things you cannot see or touch are also part of culture. They include spiritual beliefs, government, and ideas about right and wrong. Language is a very important part of culture.

Geographers want to know how the environment affects culture. Japan is a nation of mountainous islands, with very little farmland. So the Japanese use the sea for food. But the same environment may not lead to the same culture. Greece is also made of mountainous islands. The Greeks eat some fish. But they use mountainsides to get food. Goats and sheep graze there and provide food for the Greeks. ✓

The **cultural landscape** varies from place to place. In Indonesia, farmers have used technology to carve terraces into hillsides. On the plains of northern India, farmers have laid out broad, flat fields.

The Development of Culture

Scientists think that early cultures went through four important steps. First was the invention of tools. Second was the control of fire. Third was the beginnings of farming. Fourth was the development of **civilizations**.

Reading Check

Describe the way environment affects culture.

Vocabulary Strategy

The word *landscape* has more than one meaning. You may already know one of its meanings. Circle the words in the bracketed paragraph that are context clues for *landscape*. What does it mean in this context?

Key Terms

culture (KUL chur) *n.* the way of life of a people, including their beliefs and practices

cultural landscape (KUL chur ul LAND skayp) *n.* the parts of a people's environment that they have shaped and the technology they have used to shape it

civilization (sih vuh luh ZAY shun) *n.* an advanced culture with cities and a system of writing

Early people were hunters and gatherers. They traveled from place to place. As they traveled, they collected wild plants, hunted animals, and fished. Later, they learned to grow crops. They tamed wild animals to help them work or to use for food. Over time, people got more of their food from farming. This is called the Agricultural Revolution.

Farmers were able to grow more food than they needed. This meant that some people could work full time on crafts such as metalworking. They traded the things they made for food. People developed laws and government. To keep track of things, they developed writing. All these events together created the first civilizations. That was about 5,000 years ago. ✓

In time, farming and civilization spread throughout the world. Then, about 200 years ago, people invented power-driven machinery. This was the beginning of the Industrial Revolution. It led to the growth of cities, science, and highly advanced technologies.

Before the Agricultural Revolution, people had simple **institutions**. These were extended families and simple political institutions, such as councils of elders. As people gathered in larger groups, they needed more complex institutions. They developed religions. States needed schools, armies and governments. Today, we have many different kinds of institutions. They help to organize our culture.

Review Questions

1. List the events that led to the first civilizations.

_____

_____

2. What are two events of the Agricultural Revolution?

_____

_____

✓ Reading Check

What happened because farmers were able to grow more food than they needed?

_____

_____

_____

Target Reading Skill

What invention led to the Industrial Revolution?

_____

_____

Key Term

institution (in stuh TOO shun) *n.* a custom or organization with social, educational, or religious purposes

Prepare to Read

Section 2 Culture and Society

Objectives

1. Learn how people are organized into groups.
2. Look at language.
3. Explore the role of religion.

Target Reading Skill

Understand Sequence Throughout history, things change. You can show a sequence of changes by simply listing the changes. As you read this section, list some of the changes that have happened in societies. Here is an example for you.

<u>Extended family</u> **changed to** <u>nuclear family</u>

Vocabulary Strategy

Use Context to Clarify Meaning Social studies textbooks often contain words that are new to you. These textbooks have context clues to help you figure out the meanings of words. Context refers to the words and sentences just before and after each new word. The clues can include examples, explanations, or definitions. As you read, use the graphic organizer as a guide to help you find the meaning of new words.

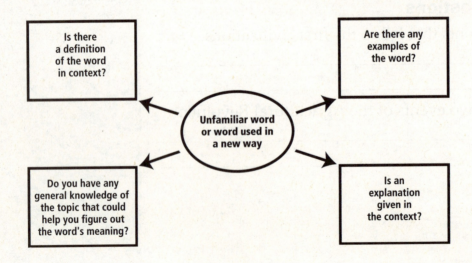

42 Reading and Vocabulary Study Guide

Section 2 Summary

How Society Is Organized

A group of people who share a culture is known as a **society**. A society may be as small as a single community. Or it may be as large as a nation. It may even be a group of nations. Every society has a **social structure**. Smaller groups in a society work together. For example, teachers, doctors, and farmers are part of the social structure. Social structure helps people work together to meet basic needs.

The family is the basic, most important part of every society. Families teach the customs and traditions of the culture to their children. ✓

[Society is also organized into **social classes**. A person's place in society may come from wealth, land, ancestors, or education. In the past, it was often hard for people to move from one social class to another. Today, people in many societies can improve their position in society. They can get a good education, make more money, or marry into a higher class.

In some cultures, people think of family as a mother, father, and children. The **nuclear family** is common in the United States.

Other cultures have **extended families**. In addition to the parents and children, there are the children's wives and husbands. It also includes the children's children. In extended families, older people often help care for the children. They are respected for their knowledge and experience. They pass on traditions. Extended families are not as common as they once were. As people move to cities, nuclear families are becoming more common.

✓ Reading Check

What is the most important part of any society?

_____

_____

Target Reading Skill

In the past, it was hard for people to move from one social class to another. Read the bracketed paragraph to find out if that has changed. Has it? How?

_____

_____

_____

Key Terms

society (suh SY uh tee) *n.* a group of people sharing a culture
social structure (SOH shul STRUK chur) *n.* a pattern of organized relationships among groups of people within a society
social class (SOH shul klas) *n.* a grouping of people based on rank or status
nuclear family (NOO klee ur FAM uh lee) *n.* a mother, a father, and their children
extended family (ek STEN did FAM uh lee) *n.* a family that includes several generations

Language

All cultures have language. Cultures depend on language. People learn their cultures through language. ✓

Language describes the things that are important to that culture. For example, English has words for Christian and Jewish beliefs. Other languages do not have words for these beliefs because their speakers are not Christian or Jewish. But they have words for the beliefs of their religion.

In some countries, people speak more than one language. Canada has two official languages, English and French. In the United States, you usually hear English, but you can also hear Spanish, Chinese, and other languages. India has 16 official languages, but people there speak more than 800 languages!

A country can have more than one culture when its people speak different languages. This is because they may have different festivals or different customs. They talk about different things.

Religion

Religion is another important part of every culture. It helps people make sense of the world. It provides comfort and hope in hard times. It helps answer questions about life and death. And it guides people in ethics, or how to act toward others. People of the same religion may practice their religion differently. ✓

Religious beliefs vary. Members of some religions believe in one God. Members of others believe in more than one god. But all religions have prayers and rituals. Every religion celebrates important places and times. All religions expect people to treat one another well and to behave properly.

Review Questions

1. What is the difference between an extended family and a nuclear family?

2. What do all religions expect people to do?

Reading Check

Why is language an important part of culture?

Vocabulary Strategy

What does the word *ethics* mean? Use the graphic organizer on page 42 to help you figure out what it means. Then write a definition below.

Reading Check

Why is religion important to people?

CHAPTER 4

Prepare to Read

Section 3 Cultural Change

Objectives

1. Explore how cultures change.
2. Learn how ideas spread from one culture to another.

Target Reading Skill

Recognize Words That Signal Sequence Signal words are words or phrases that prepare you for what is coming next. They are like following the directions in a recipe for baking a cake. When baking, you need to pay attention to the order of when ingredients are added, how long to mix or bake, and when to ask an adult to take something out of the oven.

When you read, look for words such as *first*, *next*, *then*, *later*, *before*, or *at that time*. They signal the order in which the events took place.

Vocabulary Strategy

Use Context to Clarify Meaning Sometimes you may read a word you recognize, but you aren't sure about its meaning. Many words have more than one meaning. What a word means depends on its context. Look for clues in the surrounding words or sentences. For example, the word *matter* has many meanings. You will find what meaning the author had in mind by looking at the context.

Some examples of *matter* are listed in the chart below.

Word	Definitions	Examples
matter	what all things are made of	It was made up of organic matter.
	subject of concern	It was a personal matter.
	material that is spoken or written	This package contains only printed matter.
	trouble	What is the matter?
	to be important	My grades matter to me.

Chapter 4 Section 3 **45**

Section 3 Summary

How Cultures Change

All cultures change over time. Just look at the culture of blue jeans. They were invented in the United States. At first, only Americans wore them. But today, jeans are popular all over the world. This culture of clothing changed.

Cultures are always changing. Culture is an entire way of life. A change in one part changes other parts. Changes in the natural environment, technology, and ideas all affect culture.

New technologies change a culture. During the 1800s and early 1900s, industry grew and factories spread. Americans moved from the countryside to the cities. Because people had to walk to work, they had to live close to the factories. Cities grew as a result.

The invention of the car in the late 1800s changed all this. By 1920, many Americans had cars. People could live farther from their jobs and drive to work. The idea of owning a house with a yard became more popular. That led to the growth of suburbs since the mid-1900s. A new culture based on car travel began. ✓

Technology has changed the culture in other ways. Radio and television brought entertainment and news into homes. Today, instant information is part of our culture. Computers change how and where people work. They even help people live longer. Doctors use computers to treat patients.

Cultural change has been going on for a long time. Controlling fire helped people survive colder climates. When people started to farm, they could stay in one place. Before that, they moved about in search of wild plants and animals.

How Ideas Spread

The airplane has made it easier for people to move all over the world. When they move, they bring new kinds of clothing and tools with them. They also bring new ideas.

✓ Reading Check

How did the invention of cars change culture?

_____
_____
_____

Target Reading Skill

What do the words *Before that*, in the bracketed paragraph, tell you about the sequence of events? Place the events in the paragraph in the order they took place.

1. _____
2. _____
3. _____

Ideas can travel to new places in other ways. People may buy something from another culture then learn to make it themselves. They may learn from other cultures through written matter. This movement of customs and ideas is called **cultural diffusion**.

Baseball began as an American sport, but today it is played all over the world. That is an example of cultural diffusion. The Japanese love baseball. But they have changed the game to fit their culture. These changes are an example of **acculturation**. Americans value competition. They focus on winning. A baseball game isn't over until one team wins. In Japan, a game can end in a tie. The Japanese focus on how well the game is played, not on winning.

For thousands of years, cultures changed slowly. People, ideas, and goods moved by foot, or wagon, or boat. Now things go much faster. Faxes and computers send information almost instantly. Magazines and television bring ideas and information from all over the world to any home. When ideas are shared quickly, culture changes quickly. ✓

Change can help, but it can also hurt. If things change too fast, people may feel that they are losing their culture. It is hard to bring back lost traditions. People are working to preserve their own cultures before it is too late. They want to save their artistic traditions, religious beliefs, and wisdom for future generations.

Review Questions

1. How did the car change where people live?

_____

_____

2. List two ways in which ideas travel from one culture to another.

_____

_____

Key Terms
cultural diffusion (KUL chur ul dih FYOO zhun) *n.* the movement of customs and ideas
acculturation (uh kul chur AY shun) *n.* the process of accepting new ideas and fitting them into a culture

Vocabulary Strategy

The word *matter* is used in the underlined sentence. Find it and circle it. How is it used here? Copy the correct definition from the chart at the beginning of this section.

_____

_____

_____

✓ Reading Check

Why do ideas spread faster today?

_____

_____

_____

Chapter 4 Assessment

1. Ideas and ways of doing things are called
   A. environment.
   B. cultural traits.
   C. cultural landscape.
   D. institutions.

2. What is the name for the change from hunting and gathering to growing more food than farmers need?
   A. the Invention of Tools
   B. the Agricultural Revolution
   C. the Development of Civilizations
   D. the Industrial Revolution

3. What is the most important part of every society?
   A. social classes
   B. governments
   C. the family
   D. nations

4. People learn their cultures mainly through
   A. schools.
   B. government.
   C. religion.
   D. language.

5. Which of the following cultural changes is a result of the invention of the car?
   A. the growth of suburbs
   B. the move from the countryside to the nation's cities
   C. the loss of valuable traditions
   D. the speeding up of cultural change

Short Answer Question

Explain how playing baseball in Japan is an example of acculturation.

_____
_____
_____
_____

CHAPTER 5

Prepare to Read

Section 1 Natural Resources

Objectives

1. Learn about natural resources.
2. Investigate energy.

Target Reading Skill

Identify Main Ideas Good readers look for the main idea of what they read. The main idea is the most important point. It is the one that includes all the other points, or details. Sometimes the main idea is stated in a sentence at the beginning, middle, or end of the paragraph.

The headings in a textbook give you information about the main idea. Think about the headings as you read the section. Try turning headings into questions to help you find the main idea. As you read, ask yourself, "What is this about?"

The first heading on the next page is What Are Natural Resources? Which of the sentences that follow the heading is the main idea? *Hint:* It is the sentence that answers the question that the heading asks.

Vocabulary Strategy

Using Word Origins Many English words are made from Greek roots, or word parts. When scientists need a new word they often use Greek roots.

In this chapter, you will read the word *geothermal*. It is made up of two Greek roots:

geo (from *gaia*, which means *earth*) + *therm* (which means *heat*)

Now that you know its Greek roots, can you figure out what *geothermal* means?

Other English words that are related to these Greek roots are *geography*, and *thermostat*. See if you can answer this. What is the name of the instrument a doctor uses to see how high your temperature is when you have a fever?

Chapter 5 Section 1 **49**

Section 1 Summary

What Are Natural Resources?

Everything that people use is made with **natural resources**. Natural resources are things like water, minerals, and plants.

People use some resources just as they are found in nature. Fresh water is one of these. But most resources must be changed first. Resources that must be changed or worked are called **raw materials**. For example, trees are the raw materials for paper and wood.

The world is filled with natural resources. But not all resources are alike. There are two main groups.

Renewable resources can be replaced. Some are replaced naturally because of the way Earth works. Water is one of these. Earth has a steady supply of water because of the water cycle.

[Some types of energy are renewable resources. Solar energy is a renewable resource. No matter how much of the sun's energy we use, there will always be more. The same is true for geothermal energy.

Living things such as plants and animals are also renewable resources. With proper planning, people can have a steady supply of living resources. For example, timber companies can plant new trees to replace the ones they cut down.

The second major group of resources is called **nonrenewable resources**. They include most nonliving things, such as metal ores, most minerals, natural gas, and petroleum. These cannot be replaced. Coal, natural gas, and petroleum are called fossil fuels. Scientists think they were created from the remains of prehistoric living things. In time, these fuels will run out. ✓

Key Terms

natural resources (NACH ur ul REE sawr siz) *n.* useful materials found in the environment

raw materials (raw muh TIHR ee ulz) *n.* natural resources that must be worked to be useful

renewable resources (rih NOO uh bul REE sawr siz) *n.* natural resources that can be replaced

nonrenewable resources (nahn rih NOO uh bul REE sawr siz) *n.* natural resources that cannot be replaced

---

Target Reading Skill

Which sentence directly states the main idea of the bracketed paragraph? Circle the sentence.

✓ Reading Check

What is the difference between renewable and nonrenewable resources?

_____

_____

However, many metals, minerals, and plastics can be recycled. The resource can be reused. The material hasn't been replaced, but recycling means we will use less of the resource.

A Special Resource: Energy

Many natural resources are sources of energy. People use energy from fossil fuels. They also use energy from the wind and the sun. Dams use the power of falling water to make hydroelectric power.

People in every country need energy. But energy resources are not spread evenly around the world. Some areas have many energy resources. Others have few.

Countries like Canada and Saudi Arabia have more energy resources than they need. They sell some to other countries. Countries like Japan and the United States cannot make as much energy as they use. They have to buy energy from other countries. ✓

Every day, people use more and more energy. There are not enough fossil fuels to meet energy needs in the future. This means that people will have to find other kinds of energy.

[Here are some ideas. Wind and solar energy are available. Geothermal energy is energy from the heat of Earth's interior. It will not run out. Biomass, or plant material, is a renewable source of energy.]

Atomic energy uses radioactive materials. They are not renewable, but they are plentiful. Radioactive materials can be dangerous. On the other hand, atomic energy does not pollute the air.

Fossil fuels will last longer if people use less energy. New technologies can help. You may have seen hybrid cars. They use less gas. If people use less energy now, there will be more energy in the future.

Review Questions

1. Why are trees considered a renewable resource?

_____

_____

2. List two ways that people can use less energy.

_____

_____

✓ Reading Check

Why do some countries have to buy energy?

_____

_____

_____

Vocabulary Strategy

The word *energy* comes from a Greek root that means *work* or *activity*. The bracketed paragraph describes several different kinds of energy. Pick one and write a sentence that describes how that form of energy works for us.

_____

_____

_____

_____

Prepare to Read

Section 2 Land Use

Objectives

1. Study the link between land use and culture.
2. Investigate the link between land use and economic activity.
3. Explore changes in land use.

Target Reading Skill

Identify Supporting Details The main idea of a paragraph or section is its most important point. The main idea is supported by details. Details explain the main idea. They may give additional facts or examples. They can tell you *what*, *where*, *why*, *how much*, or *how many*.

In the second paragraph on the next page, the first sentence states the main idea:

Even in similar environments, people may use land differently.

To find the details, ask yourself, "*How* do people use land differently?"

Vocabulary Strategy

Using Word Origins Many English words came from other languages. For example, many words have been made by combining Latin word parts. In fact, all of the key terms in this section are based on Latin words. We will look at one of them now. You can use a dictionary to find the Latin word parts of the others.

Let's take a closer look at the word *manufacturing*. It is made up of two Latin word parts:

manu ("hand") + *factura* ("making")

To manufacture means to make something by hand. What do you call a place where things are manufactured? *Hint:* The word begins with the Latin word part for *making*.

Section 2 Summary

Land Use and Culture

How people use their land depends on their culture. People may use land differently because their cultures have developed in different **environments**. The Inuit live in a cold, arctic climate. It is too cold to grow crops. The Inuit use their land mainly for hunting wild animals. The Japanese live in a warmer, wetter climate. Their main crop is rice. It grows well in Japan's climate.

Even in similar environments, people may use land differently. That is because they have different cultural traits. Georgia has a climate like Japan. But farmers in Georgia don't grow rice. Instead, Georgians raise chickens and grow crops like peanuts. The Japanese eat rice at nearly every meal. But Americans eat more meat and peanut butter. ✓

Cultures change landscapes. Thousands of years ago, Western Europe was covered with forests. Then farming cultures began to spread across the region. People cleared forests to use the land for farming. Today, most of the land is open fields and pastures.

Different cultures respond differently to their environments. Much of the western United States has a dry climate. People use pipes and sprinklers to water crops. The Middle East also has a dry climate. But Middle Eastern farmers use qanats, or brick irrigation channels, to water their crops. Both cultures live in similar environments. But they do things differently.

Land Use and Economic Activity

There are three ways of making a living. Geographers have grouped these ways into three stages or levels.

[In the first stage, people use land and resources directly to make products. They may hunt, cut wood, mine, or fish. They may herd animals or raise crops. Most of the world's land is used for first-level activities. In developed countries, such as the United States, only a few people make a living in this way.] ✓

Key Term
environment (en VY run munt) *n.* natural surroundings

✓ Reading Check
Even though the climate in Georgia is good for growing rice, farmers in Georgia don't grow rice. Why?

_____
_____
_____

Target Reading Skill
List three details in the bracketed paragraph about first-level activities.

1. _____
2. _____
3. _____

✓ Reading Check
How is most of the world's land used?

_____
_____
_____

Vocabulary Strategy

The word *automobile* combines the Greek word *auto* ("self") and the Latin word *mobile* ("to move"). Try this one yourself. If a biography is the story of someone's life, what is an *autobiography*?

_____
_____
_____

✓ Reading Check

How did European colonization change the American landscape?

_____
_____
_____

At the second stage, people process the products of the first-level activities. For example, they turn trees into lumber, or wool from sheep into sweaters. Most second-level activity is **manufacturing**. Manufacturing is important in developed countries, especially in cities.

Third-level activities are also known as services. While services do not produce goods, services may help deliver or sell goods. Many businesses offer services. They include doctors, bankers, automobile repair workers, and clerks. Services are often found in cities, especially in developed countries.

Changes in Land Use

During **colonization**, the newcomers may change the landscape. If farmers move to an area without farms, they will create farms. As people find new ways of making a living, they will start using the land in new ways, too.

Crops such as wheat and grapes were unknown in the Americas before colonization. So were animals such as cows and chickens. When Europeans came, they cleared large areas for their crops and animals. ✓

Since the 1800s, **industrialization** has changed landscapes in many countries. Cities have grown around factories. Since 1900, suburbs have spread. The spread of cities and suburbs is known as sprawl.

Review Questions

1. What are second-level activities?

_____
_____

2. How are second-level activities different from third-level activities?

_____
_____

Key Terms
manufacturing (man yoo FAK chur ing) *n.* the large-scale production of goods by hand or by machine
colonization (kahl uh nuh ZAY shun) *n.* the movement of settlers and their culture to a new country
industrialization (in dus tree ul ih ZAY shun) *n.* the growth of machine-powered production in an economy

Prepare to Read

Section 3
People's Effect on the Environment

Objectives

1. Investigate how first-level activities affect the environment.
2. Explore how second- and third-level activities affect the environment.

Target Reading Skill

Identify Implied Main Ideas Have you ever had a conversation with someone where you had to pay close attention to what they were saying? Maybe they were telling you all the details about a family event, but what they were actually talking about was how important their family is to them.

Sometimes reading is like that. The main idea is not stated directly. Instead, the details in a paragraph or section add up to a main idea. In a case like this, we say the main idea is implied. It is up to you to put the details together. You will then be able to see the main idea.

For example, the details in the first paragraph on the next page add up to this main idea:

First-level activities are necessary for human survival, but they reshape the environment.

Vocabulary Strategy

Using Word Origins Many English words have been made from Greek word parts. Some of these word parts are names for new inventions. For example, the ancient Greeks used the word part "tele" to mean *far off*. They used the word part "phone" to mean *sound*. We put those word parts together to give us *telephone*. Now that is something the ancient Greeks never imagined!

There are many other words that use each of these roots. Below is a partial list.

telecommunication	telescope
telecommute	television
telegraph	headphone
telemarketing	microphone

Chapter 5 Section 3 **55**

Section 3 Summary

First-Level Activities

In first-level activities people use raw materials to get food and resources to live. In the process the environment changes. For example, crops replace wild plants.

As countries grow, new ways of farming are tried. In the Great Plains of North America, farms have replaced land where buffalo roamed. In the Netherlands, people have drained wetlands to create dry farmland. Creating new farmland destroyed wild grasslands and wetlands. But the new land has fed millions of people. ✓

Agriculture, forestry, and fishing provide resources that people need to live. But they sometimes hurt the environment. Wood is needed to build houses. But cutting down too many trees can lead to **deforestation**. Animals that depend on the forest may also suffer. Deforestation can lead to a loss of **biodiversity**.

Farmers use fertilizers to grow crops. More people can be fed. But rain washes the chemicals into streams. This harms fish and the people who eat the fish.

The key is to find a balance. Around the world, people are working to find ways of meeting their needs without hurting the environment. One way is to plant tree farms. Or farmers can use natural methods to grow crops. Or they can use chemicals that will not damage waterways. Fishers can catch fish that are more plentiful.

Second- and Third-Level Activities

Over the years industry, or second-level activities, and services, or third-level activities have changed deserts, prairies, and forests. These activities have created a landscape of cities, factories, offices, highways, and shopping malls.

✓ Reading Check

What is one way people have created new farmland?

_____
_____
_____

Target Reading Skill

In one sentence, state what all the details in the bracketed paragraph are about.

_____
_____

Key Terms

deforestation (dee fawr uh STAY shun) *n.* a loss of forest cover in a region

biodiversity (by oh duh VUR suh tee) *n.* a richness of different kinds of living things in a region

Industrial and service activities provide most of the jobs in developed countries. The main purpose of some of these activities is to change the environment. **Civil engineering** builds structures that change the landscape. For example, dams create lakes that cover large areas with water. They provide water for farms and cities. They also protect areas from flooding.

Other industrial and service activities have side effects on the environment. Industries use large amounts of resources. They release industrial wastes into the environment. Service activities require the building of roads, telephone lines, and power lines. ✓

Industry is not the only source of **pollution**. Our own trash may pollute the soil, water, or air. Exhaust from cars and trucks causes air pollution. Air pollution may cause harmful changes in our climate.

Working together, people can find solutions to these problems. One is to use more fuel-efficient cars. Cars that burn less fuel create less air pollution. Renewable energy resources pollute less than fossil fuels.

Waste can be recycled to reduce the amount that must be burned or dumped. It also saves natural resources. For example, paper can be recycled. Then fewer trees have to be cut down to make new paper.

Finding ways to solve environmental problems is one of the greatest challenges of our time.

✓ Reading Check

How do industrial activities affect the environment?

_____
_____

Vocabulary Strategy

The word *industry* comes from the Latin word *industrius* ("hard working"). What does it mean to say that someone is industrious?

_____
_____

Review Questions

1. How does deforestation hurt the environment?

_____
_____

2. List ways in which industrial and service activities change landscapes.

_____
_____

Key Terms

civil engineering (SIV ul en juh NIHR ing) *n.* technology for building structures that alter the landscape, such as dams, roads, and bridges

pollution (puh LOO shun) *n.* waste, usually man-made, that makes the air, water, or soil less clean

Chapter 5 Assessment

1. Resources that must be worked are called
   A. renewable resources.
   B. nonrenewable resources.
   C. recyclable materials.
   D. raw materials.

2. Which of the following is a renewable resource?
   A. water
   B. metal ore
   C. natural gas
   D. coal

3. Manufacturing is an example of
   A. a first-level activity.
   B. a second-level activity.
   C. a third-level activity.
   D. all of the above

4. Cutting down too many trees can lead to
   A. biodiversity.
   B. deforestation.
   C. pollution.
   D. loss of biomass.

5. In developed countries, most of the jobs are in
   A. agriculture.
   B. first-level activities.
   C. industrial and service activities.
   D. first- and third-level activities.

Short Answer Question

List three ways that people affect the environment.

_____
_____
_____